To Jerry

A FAMILIAR STRANGER

With Love

A FAMILIAR STRANGER

MATTHEW WILLIAMS

Published in paperback in 2019 by Sixth Element Publishing
on behalf of Matthew Williams

Sixth Element Publishing
Arthur Robinson House
13-14 The Green
Billingham TS23 1EU
Tel: 01642 360253
www.6epublishing.net

ISBN 978-1-912218-78-3

British Library Cataloguing in Publication Data. A catalogue record for this
book is available from the British Library.

Printed in Great Britain.

For everybody that's been there

CONTENTS

LIVING

a guide to modern living

contribute to the economy
look good while doing it

#7 sins - envy

the fuel that powers
the capitalist dream
stoked by advertisers
who want us to feel
that we are worth it
we mustn't miss out
persuade us our value
lies not within
but without
a rampant social virus
transmitted via screens
symptoms alleviated, briefly
by a shot of dopamine
administered in shops
while we're filling up the tills
buoying the emerging market
in anti-depressant pills

us vs them

we measure and compare
our lives against theirs
our insides versus their outsides
the highlights that are shared
and always we fall short
of a victory no-one can claim
because behind the smiles
and the perfect lives
inside we're all the same

fuck comparison

too fat
too skinny
too old
too wrinkly
too unattractive
too unathletic
too stupid
too pathetic

constant comparison
always too little
constant battering
of self-worth so brittle
constant spotlight
revealing all that you're not

fuck comparison

show the world
what you've got

#7 sins - greed

wanting more
never enough
wanting more
endless stuff
wanting more
fuelling growth
wanting more
keeps the market afloat
wanting more
shit you don't need
wanting more
the modern creed

#7 sins - pride

vulgar displays
of status and wealth
worshipping at
the temple of self
sculpting monuments
to vanity
flawless complexions
lithe bodies
airbrushed and filtered
nipped and tucked
anything to achieve
that perfect look
and beneath the edifice
these totems to pride
buried are the fears
the illusion hides

ambition

anything is possible
what a time to be alive
abundant opportunities
to make your mark and thrive
shattering glass ceilings
pushing boundaries, breaking new ground
scaling new heights of ambition
nothing can keep you down
you can be a gp or a surgeon
mp or ceo
head teacher, chief inspector
there's no limit to how far you can go
an artist or a poet
you could take to the stage and sing
but in a world where you can be anything
the best you can be
is thin

bully

a swinging brick
where a heart should be
rampaging ego
me, me, me
riding roughshod
tearing up rules
don't care who's subjected to
your tirades of abuse
full of self-importance
fuck everybody else
mere puppets of your ambition
make their lives a living hell
heaping pressure until they crumble
broken, beat and scarred
you climb atop the rubble
it got you where you are

sorry

own your mistakes
take responsibility
admit when you're wrong
accept culpability
hold your hands up
say you're sorry
take it on the chin
it isn't always someone else's fault
nor a battle that you must win

modern languages

emerging blue sky thinking
cultivated outside of the box
innovation, added value
a pair of wacky socks
deep diving, mining insight
evolving ideas, synergy

what the hell you talking about
sounds like bollocks to me

on hold

hello and how may we help you
we're placing you in a queue
we value your call so please hold on
here's some music to hum along to

you've come through to the wrong department
please may i have your name
your house number and your post code
and your date of birth
(again)

i'm sorry i didn't quite catch that
could you please repeat it for me
try to speak clearly and please don't swear
our lines are incredibly busy

maybe one day you'll get lucky
and get a human on the end of the line
in the meantime we appreciate your patience
while we continue to waste your time

patience

patience seeps
an emptying cup
a distant virtue
left behind
in the rush

#7 sins - anger

go home
don't take what's mine
you're not welcome here

go faster
get the hell out of my way
put your foot down or steer clear

who the fuck do you think you are
telling me what to do
you ain't no better than me you twat
to hell with you
fuck you

and all you benefits scroungers
freeloading while i graft
get off your lazy arses and work
stop sponging off my tax

lying, thieving politicians
with your snouts buried in the trough
you don't represent the common man
stuck-up entitled toffs

lashing out in all directions
fire and fury aflame in the breast
one day the house of cards will burn
in the wrath of the dispossessed

#7 sins - sloth

shiftless, lazy, good for nuthin'
sitting on your arse
contributing nothing
no endeavour, no end product
no labour, no honest toil
a waste of space on minimum wage
while others share the spoils

a deadened mind killing company time
in a dead-end job
nine-to-five
day after day after endless day
monotony, monotony
then more of the same

filling others' pockets
a cog in the machine
wasting away
in a bullshit job
in the capitalist game

aggro

rude, obnoxious, think you're the shit
boorish, full of it, you arrogant git
think you're the bollocks
but act like a tit
all tough talk no trousers
you total fucking dick
looking to cause some aggro
cos you can't handle your drink
be the big man in your own little world
and leave me be
you prick

pause, press play

learn from the past
but don't live there
pay it forward
don't play it back
life has no stop or rewind button
just a single continuous track

take pause

reflect when needed
you could have done things
a different way
but don't be consumed
by reproach and regret
just do better
next time you press play

rat race

sounds so easy when you say it
'live one day at a time'
in practice it's not so simple
caught up in hectic lives
so much shit to think about
people to see and things to do
worries about the future
plans to follow through
drifting away from the moment
heads float off into space
and the present that's right here right now
left trailing in the rat race

priorities

rich or poor
you can't buy time
use it wisely
there's a finite supply
what is it that really matters
can those notifications wait
to whose tune are you dancing
supplicating to others' dictates
who care not for your happiness
won't be there when chips are down
won't be there for your children
when the pressures on you mount
keep sight of what's important
to you and those you love
don't let your life pass you by
dealing with everyone else's stuff

golden years

when did we lose reverence
for the precious treasures of time
years etched onto faces
weathered by the seasons of life

in the golden years that are promised to few
why do we fight to cling onto
the fruits of a youth for which we never paid dues
a denial of the years that have made us who
we are today full of wisdom accrued
lessons learned to pass onto
a new generation that follows us through
as nature ever intended it to

youth is nature's decree
not a product to buy
a flame that burns briefly
in all gifted life
now it's time once again
to wear age with pride
embrace the twilight
don't let it slip by
believing the rubbish
we're constantly sold
don't allow age
to be wasted on the old

compassion fatigue

it's much easier to sit and judge
than to try and understand
far simpler to dismiss and condemn
than to offer a helping hand
more convenient to blame the victim
look down our noses from on high
than it is for us to remember
there but for the grace of god
go i

impossible

dream with your eyes open
paddle against the tide
the impossible becomes the inevitable
when ideas alight on their time

that's living online

information overload
data, facts and lies
fake news, memes and cat videos
filters erasing lines
adverts adverts adverts
so much shit to buy
causes seeking your support
'share this or else he'll die'

facebook, insta, twitter
snapchat, tinder, pof
windows to the modern world
but what is true and what is false

a trade in electro currency
of comments, likes and shares
between connections, friends and followers
but when you need them
who'll be there

a sea of choices

paralysed by choices
how to know which one is right
when faced with so many options
frozen by fear that i might
make the wrong selection
fear of missing out
on all of the alternatives
filling me with doubt
no confidence in my decisions
so many possibilities abound
scared to make a commitment
and in a sea of choice
i drown

the great delusion

clinging tightly to an illusion
too afraid to let it go
unsettled by uncertainty
terrified of the unknown
thirsting for power, for agency
unable to rest until
everything is just as you want it to be
bent to the dictates of your will
squaring up for an unwinnable battle
events conspire to rip away
all that your ego desired
in a heartbeat your whole life can change
no-one is immune to the cruelties
of illness, heartbreak and loss
of loneliness, grief and hardship
we all must bear our cross
but we can choose to carry the burden
with grace and with dignity
knowing to no-one is anything owed
and it's acceptance that will set us free

a social animal

a social animal
seeks its tribe
a sense of belonging
an identity
a hive
a place that confers status
on each part of the larger whole
uniting individual actors
behind a common goal
a unifying vision
passion for a shared cause
unleashing the power to emancipate
and march us into war

this is me

persecuted for being different
not fitting an accepted norm
judged on a single characteristic
punished for how you were born
seeking a sense of belonging
a community you can call home
a tribe in which you're welcome
not facing life alone
a place of love not of hatred
where you're not tolerated
you can just be
free to unleash your potential
proud to say
this is me

time to talk

it's time to talk
time to make some noise
time to stand up and be counted
it's time to raise our voice
time for us to be noticed
to ruffle some feathers, make some waves
time to join together
we won't back down, we won't go away
we will talk until you listen
keep talking when our faces turn blue
keep talking until we see action
only then is the time to talk through

LOVING

happiness

achievement and applause
'friends' and likes
the chemical charge of consumption
pleasures that pale in the shadow
of connections forged
in the beating
of another human heart

paradox

how is it that
the way you tap tap tap
on my arm
can be both a minor irritation
and one of the reasons
i love you so much

from the heart

the heart is a curious muscle
its power pumps blood through our veins
but unlike other muscles
when hardened its strength fades away

a fierce heart is supple
it bestows the greatest of gifts
love
kindness
compassion
forgiveness

no greater strength exists

caution, hot

approaching the flame
fear ignites
but if we never enter the fire
how will we ever know
just how brightly
we can burn

#7 sins - lust

aching   burning
        scratching   tearing
            temptation   by sensation
                        intense
        visceral   consuming
                losing
        the self
            in another's   flesh
                    but never
                        in their
                            soul

intoxicating

and though she was
intoxicating
i never was at my best
when drunk

losing myself

somewhere along the way
to finding you
i found myself
losing me

how could you

never thought you would do that
couldn't be the person i knew
the one i gave my heart to
who was that if it wasn't you

what happened to the person i thought you were
before the veil was ripped from my eyes
revealing colours you'd never shown me before
shades that you'd chosen to hide

how were you able to do that
after all that we'd been through
did what we once have mean nothing
was there any of it that was true

one day you'll be just a memory
a stranger who once crossed my way
a painful lesson i needed to learn
to become the man i am today

a man who knows his own value
won't settle for less than he's worth
won't accept scraps from anyone's table
but will hold out for what he deserves

a once familiar stranger

just a once familiar stranger
somebody that i used to know
a visitor from a foreign land
where once you felt like home
yesterday we travelled in tandem
today i walk alone
each step i take leading me
further into the unknown
and maybe i could have done better
but hindsight can't be bought
now i see you and i wonder
was it a delusion
in which i was caught

i see you

i see you

i hear what you say
i read what you write
but i see

what you conceal
you reveal
what you hide
i seek

answers

revealed not in words
but in the silences
i hear

and now
i see

you

you were there all along

back to me

where once there was you
there is a space

wide
empty
where silence
echoes

a vacuum that calls to be filled
a missing piece
that need seeks to replace

searching
in all the wrong places

and with every disappointment
every bruise
each road leads back
here

to me

disconnect

when the world is at your fingertips
where does the heart
find its home

dating scene investigation

didn't know i'd need to be a detective
to try and make sense of this scene
questioning everyone's motives
never knowing who or what to believe
realising that all too often
things are not quite as they seem
and when the lies and alibis are uncovered
the perp is nowhere to be seen

does nothing mean anything anymore

sick and tired of fleeting acquaintances
that as sure as they come will go
'oh it's not personal it's just dating'
does nothing mean anything anymore
so stupid to think it could be different
that one day something could last
can't entertain the possibility
lest the remaining shards
are smashed

a sleight of heart

was i but a mere prop
in an illusion
a willing accomplice
to a sleight of heart

talking shite

anyone can say
any old shite
try to convince us
that black is white
and how many of us
will lend an ear
when the shite they talk
is what we want to hear

referee

need a referee to arbitrate
between my heart and my head
make me see reality
not fall for all that's said
so freely in the heat of the moment
empty words divorced from deeds
to remind me that actions say everything
and even the sweetest words can be cheap

time to go

won't stay around to watch you
slowly slip away

can't stay while your feelings
wither on the vine
wondering
what the hell to do with mine

can't stay and let my love for you
carve a hole
inside

distance

and now all that grows
between us
is distance

why

broken

by distance
timing
circumstance

pull it apart
analyse
question why

but does it matter

when broke is still broke
and what is wrong
can't be made right

pick your battles

fight to be a better person
fight to mend your broken ways
but don't ever fight
to keep someone
that doesn't want to stay

let's be friends

can't smash my heart to pieces
and in the name of friendship ask
for a few shards just to comfort you
while tearing me apart
take all i have or take nothing
there is no middle way
and don't expect me to be there for you
when you chose to walk away

(but i would)

where i am

maybe it was just
you didn't meet me
where i am

go

if it hurts
to stay
it's time
to go

turn off the lights

turn off the lights when you leave
lock the door
post through your keys
walk, and don't look back
it's over

let your tears fall freely
flush out the pain
hold tight to your resolve
it takes strength to walk away
love is never easy
at least that's what they say

until it is
that's when you stay

turn back the clock

i wish i could
turn back the clock
erase myself from your story
save you from
all of the hurt
stop your tears from falling

take my pen
and write for you
a character more deserving
then lay it down
upon your desk
so you can write your happy ending

priceless

your time
your energy
your commitment
your love
matter

invest them where
their value is known
and remember
you
matter

fuck tinder

won't pull myself apart for you
won't try to fit around what you're going through
won't contort myself trying to understand
won't reach out for you to push away my hand
won't doubt myself cos you don't want me around
won't stamp my dignity into the ground
while you try to figure out your shit
if you find the guts to face up to it

if this is what it takes
to not live my life alone
then fuck it
i'm through with the bullshit
i'd rather be on my own

we will build a wall

we will build a wall
to protect what we hold dear
build it high and build it strong
keep at bay our fears

the wall will hide our weaknesses
keep us safe from enemy attacks
from evil-doers that wish us harm
would stab us in the back

the wall will be our fortress
a refuge for precious things
that define us, make us who we are
camouflage what lies within

we build our walls resolutely
around hearts broken and bruised
but what is the cost of protection
when your wall makes a prisoner of you

hurt

to all the pain
along the way
the hurt i've taken
the hurt i gave
you are the teachers
that light the way
help it all make sense
someday

you reveal what needs
to change in me
things i need to do
to be

i only hope
the same is true
and the hurt i've caused
leads to better
for you

the dance

life is a musical thing
a rhythm to dance to
a song to sing
a symphony of many movements
of high notes and of low
i sway along with the music
and wonder
are some of us fated
to dance
alone

when people can walk away from you

when people can walk away from you
let them walk
their role in your story is done

when people can walk away from you
let them walk
look forward, it's time to move on

when people can walk away from you
let them walk
no matter the reasons why

when people can walk away from you
let them walk
closure comes from inside

when people can walk away from you
let them walk
don't chase after them, let them go

when people can walk away from you
let them walk
sometimes it's better to walk on your own

when people can walk away from you
let them walk
it wasn't meant to be

when people can walk away from you
let them walk
don't sacrifice your dignity

when people can walk away from you
let them walk
but don't hold bitterness in your heart

when people can walk away from you
let them walk
each ending is also a start

one

once we were two
now i am one
once you were here
now you are gone
once i was empty
lost and alone
now i have learned
how to be
on my own

you don't know what you don't know

it may be true
that you don't know what
you've got
'til it's gone
but sometimes you don't know
what you've missed
until it arrives

oceans

while others floated
on streams
you longed to dive
in the ocean

underneath the lamppost

underneath the lamppost
a shaft of light cuts through the dark
wrapping us both in its warming glow
our story about to start
lost upon a lengthy road
worn from our journeys to date
still daring to hope and to believe
that what led us here was fate
hearts that recognise one another
could our dreams become reality
take my hand let's walk together
find ourselves in you and me

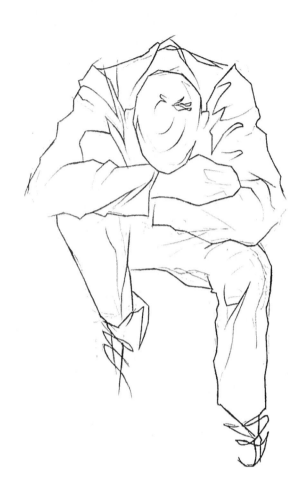

FALLING

to the baby i never knew

if fate had taken a different turn
if life had blown its breath into you
and delivered you to the world
what gifts would you have brought

would the blackness still have visited
broken down my door
would its knock have simply been delayed
same destination reached
in a different way

never got to hold you in my arms
cradle and protect you
feel your soft skin against mine
kiss you and tell you how much
daddy loves you

will never stroke your hair or scratch your back
never hold your tiny hand in mine
maybe i just wasn't ready for you
maybe it wasn't our time

my darling baby
you were a gift from god
a gift of a different kind

plasters

there is no plaster big enough
to cover a hole
in your soul

why attempt to cover
that which
screams
to be filled

tides

tides obey
the relative distances
of the earth, sun and moon

a pattern tied
to night and day
the power of the waves
swelling to the dictates
of nature's unbending rules

the waves that rise and crash
inside and all around me
to whose rhythm
do they dance

where dreams go to die

how many dreams
are laid to rest each day
by the fear of failure
and what others might say

wilderness

doubt invades, eats away
eroding confidence
desire fades
the dreams and possibilities
that energised, enthused
cloaked within the shadow
of reality's hard truths
finding myself caught between
what is
and what could be
a wilderness, a no-man's land
that drains my sense of me
a place from which i must emerge
and firmer footing find
do battle with what holds me here
the doubts
in my own mind

sleep

exhaustion seeps
into my bones
heavy eyes
long to close
beckoning sleep
to carry me away
shut out the world
erase the day

sanctuary

a longing
to close the door on the world
and retreat
to a shared sanctuary

shrinking

swimming against the current
fighting a rising tide
sliding further within myself
battling the urge to hide
to retreat from the world around me
shut this imposter away
hibernate until such time
as i am me again

silence

it follows me

its hands
rest
heavily upon my shoulders

it inhabits
the spaces i don't fill
broken
momentarily

a ticking clock
wind beating against windows
a passing car
the gurgling
of a stomach unfilled

proofs of life
puncturing

the silence

stumbling through fog

stumbling through fog
steps unsteady
lacking direction
legs feel heavy
tied to a weight
that anchors my will
resists forward motion
implores me, 'be still'
clouded in mist
that obscures the way
a claustrophobic funk
that shrouds my days
and blankets the road
that stretches ahead
feeds the fears
infesting my head
a weathered track
i must walk alone
only i can find
the way back home
to where the fog
is broken by light
my shadow cast behind me
before fading from sight

quicksand

feel the darkness closing around me
deadweight pulls me down
waist deep in this quicksand
struggling not to drown
an overwhelming instinct to hibernate
shut out the world and hide
there's no reason for me to feel this way
no sense to the turmoil inside
praying to god to cast away
this burden that i must bear
but we all have our cross to carry
and life was never meant to be fair

night

a moment…
of calm
peace

stillness

before senses awaken
and reality
crashes through the haze

trapped
in this endless night

suicide

you think that this is rational
a conscious choice that's made
with no thought to the consequences
for those left in its wake
an act of pure selfishness
by cowards that can't hack it anymore
who should be grateful and count their blessings
for all they have to be thankful for
others have it so much harder
but you don't hear them complain

before judging please consider
the nature of their pain

the agony of a suffering
remorseless in its attack
that destroys the spirit and drags us to depths
unable to see a way back
suffocating our strongest instinct
to cling onto this precious life
a pain so unrelenting
it breaks the will to survive

and to all those souls that have slipped away
taken, by their own hand
please show some compassion
please try to understand
this cruel and vicious illness
that snuffs out the light inside
shreds all sense of who we are
and offers no respite

a constant onslaught of anguish
each minute of every day
we need to talk about suicide
and end this tragic waste

where is god when it hurts

where is god when it hurts so much
when i'm lost and all alone
where is the lord of mercy
when i can't go on on my own

where is the god that loves us
each his precious child
why have i been abandoned
when i need god by my side

where is god in my hour of need
to pick me up from this fall
where is god in depression
does he hear my prayers at all

where is the god that i long for
to lift me out of this hole
where is god when i need him most
who else will save my soul

withdrawal

the world around closes in on me
nothing has changed, except chemistry
will it settle, or is this how i'll be
wish the world would pause
until i can see
if this maelstrom of emotion is temporary
as i try to find my even keel
until the storm passes please bear with me
know that i'm doing my best to deal
these cards i was given and chose to reveal
to show to others
someone knows how it feels
must never lose hope of being set free
liberated from the prison of the mind's tyranny

can't give what you don't got

love yourself like you love your children
take time to tend to your needs
don't bury them deep and neglect them
while always trying to please
for when the final page is written
and your story is all but told
there's only one character sure to be there
when the book of life is closed
always look after number one
be there for you no matter what
don't ever think that's selfish because
you can't give
what you don't got

where have all the words gone

where have all the words gone
that once tumbled from my mouth
where is it they are buried
and will they ever find their way out

where have all the words gone
that flowed effortlessly from my pen
in rhymes that poured so freely
will i ever find them again

where have all the words gone
that made me who i was
that held the key to the essence of me
where is it that my words are locked

please can i have my smile back

please can i have my smile back
and the light behind my eyes
i lost them in the thick dark fog
that surrounds me, refuses to rise

please can i have my laughter back
i've forgotten how it sounds
life isn't a life without it
please show me where it can be found

what happened to my confidence
my belief that things would work out
that i could overcome any challenge
now i'm paralysed by doubts

whatever happened to the matthew
that once occupied this space
and left but a shell, a shadow
an imposter that wears his face

i pray they'll be put back together
these pieces that have fallen apart
reassembled into a stronger whole
i pray for a new life to start

the modern sickness

listen

listen…

do you hear
what it is telling you

can you find
where your sickness
resides

in your mind

triggered by an unbalanced brain
or a normal, rational
response to the pain

inflicted
by a sick society of consumers
that consumes us

listen

listen to your pain

maybe it's trying to tell you
that you're the one
who's sane

heaven and hell

i pray
that there is a heaven
because i know
there is a hell

by your side

don't give up
a better life lies ahead
please don't give up
don't believe the lies in your head
though i know it seems impossible
for the smile to return to your face
i promise that you will get through this
i know you have what it takes
just promise me you'll keep on walking
one small step at a time
and i promise i will walk beside you
i will never leave your side

on my knees

and could it be
that what i seek
can only be found
from my knees

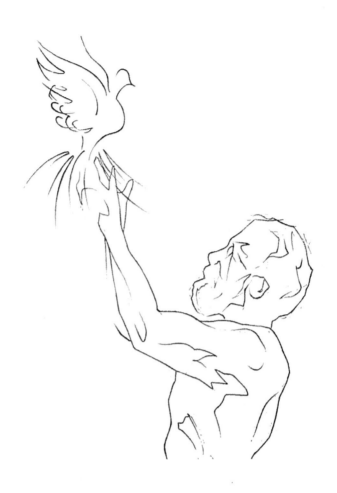

RISING

stop.

stop.
look
listen

breathe…

you are here

keep going

if you're going through hell keep on going
at the edge of the abyss don't jump
when lost in your deepest valley keep walking
you don't know when salvation will come

when the pain feels too overwhelming
and your spirit feels broken and crushed
when you no longer see a future worth living
take one more step, don't give up

as long as you breathe there is hope
for a tomorrow so much brighter than today
as long as your heart is still beating
have faith, there is always a way

if you're going through hell keep on going
hold on through the darkest of nights
your story was never meant to end here
this world still needs your light

demons

these demons
don't belong to me
they have no home here
unannounced visitors
that i never invited in
attached themselves to me
sunk in their claws
wrapped themselves around me
consuming me
refusing to release me from their grasp
but i prised them away
let them go
i don't carry the demons with me
i am free

the sun

i never dreamed
my darkest days
would lead
directly
to the sun

standing at the precipice

standing at the precipice
staring over the edge
beckoned to take that one small step
that will take you beyond the ledge

a single step once taken
that promises no return
no pause, no rewind, no regrets, no lifeline
when your final bridge has been burned

how can one ever be sure
before plunging into the unknown
while others advise they can't see what's inside
the choice is yours alone

and though there will be no going back
once your choice has been made
you must conquer your doubt
flames of fear stamp out
give yourself to the hand of fate

so to the moment of reckoning
raise your head and look to the sky
a leap of faith
grab your chance now don't wait
how else will you learn how to fly

breaking through

through the thickest of walls
the tiniest of cracks
invites
a pinhole of light
that bathes everything
in the sun's warming glow

a flick of the switch

a flick of the switch
a spark ignites
a flicker at first
now glowing bright

a flame that dances within my eyes
extinguishes dark with light
bringing calm after the raging storm
ending the darkest of nights

and as winter gives way to springtime
new seeds wait to be sown
a time for dreams to blossom
for my heart to find its home

where i'm meant to be

in search of somewhere
to belong

charting my voyage
setting the sails
trusting the movement
of the tides and the waves
for events to conspire
fall into place
arrive where i
can finally say

'this is me'

landing where
i'm meant to be

rejection

as one rejection follows another
feels like an endless parade
of disappointments and let-downs
imagined futures fade
hopes, dreams and ambitions
buried side-by-side
leave them there to rest in peace
can't resurrect what's died
can't let dreams ever unfulfilled
haunt your nights and days
cloud your vision and blind you to
opportunities that cross your way
for every slap across the face
each blow below the belt
it takes but one chance
to turn things around
and for all the dots
to connect

promise

don't allow
your doubts to steal
the promise of what
tomorrow could be

whispers

riddled and wracked
wrestling with doubt
a voice within
that doesn't scream or shout

but whispers

insistent

that there's no point
that i'm no good
that things never change
why did i ever think they would

lies fed to my psyche
by a nemesis inside
who won't be evicted
but waits
and hides

and whispers…

i hear
but i won't listen

recovery

only by reaching rock bottom
did i discover how far i could climb
only when i was broken
could i trace my mind's faultlines
only out of my doubts
could clarity emerge
only through my failures
were my greatest lessons learned

the next step

you'll never know
just how far you could go
unless you take
the next step

empty page

empty page
blank but for promise
a pen that is poised
willing words to flow from it
who knows where they're born
from which well they spring
how they bleed from the ink
and reveal what's within

illuminating emotions
buried inside
thoughts, feelings
that otherwise hide
elude my grasp
a confusing swirl
before finding their form
in the pen's smooth whirl
tracing in script
recesses of the soul
uncovering meaning
making me whole

a precious gift
this tool to unearth
the mysteries of self
revealed in the words

creativity, flair and passion

sometimes I find myself
wishing I was steady
an even keel, predictable
moods that don't shift and eddy

that my days would all be coloured
a consistent kind of hue
a more reliable temperament

'but then you wouldn't be you'

creativity, flair and passion
don't trickle steadily from the source
creative minds are rarely tidy
and from the chaos
inspiration is born

taking flight

each time i put pen to paper
send my words out into the world
a piece of myself is cast away
on the winds with wings unfurled
crossing countries, spanning oceans
no barriers impede their flight
from my soul to their destination
in the hearts of those that they find

pieces of you

share kindly with others
pieces of you
but don't give them all away
save some pieces
just for you
and always keep them safe

simple things

a clever turn of phrase

a glorious chorus
building to a magnificent crescendo

ideas that make me think
in a new way

grown men in gloves
punching each other in the face

tea and toast
a book to read
a pen to write
a kind heart
beautiful eyes

the simple things
that make me smile

peace

i searched
never knowing
what i was looking for
hoping to recognise it
when it arrived

more and more
i realise
it's not out there
but somewhere inside

a stillness

and a whisper that guides
to peace
of heart and mind

in bloom

bloom where you are planted
play the hand you're dealt
withstand the storms
for they water your soul
lead you to what you are meant
to learn so that you can grow stronger
play your hand with greater skill
and whatever you face
in this game called life
let nothing break your will
let your spirit magnify in adversity
allow shade to reveal your light
and when you reap your harvest
share it where cold winds bite

#7 sins - gluttony

my appetites are captive to a compulsion
to gorge

an ever-present hunger
an unquenchable thirst
an inordinate desire

to consume

words
ideas

and fill myself
to overflowing

rise

i have failed
i have fallen
been beaten
and broken
i've doubted
and questioned
been lost and
forsaken
i was discarded
forgotten
knocked down
but i've risen

just trying to figure this shit out

making it up as i go along
do my best to get it right

do to others as i'd have done to me
forgive myself when i am wrong
i'm working on it

take responsibility for my failures and foibles
my imperfections and faults
and if i can't change
at least be more aware

don't expect myself to be perfect
that's too great a height from which to fall

who am i
what the hell happened
what did i do
and why

i'll never have all the answers
never have it all sussed out
i'll keep walking along on my own path
just trying to figure this shit out

choices

the hand of fate
a lucky break
the love we make
and the loves
that take
the heights to which we soar
lows to which
we fall
what defines a life
are choices
above all

connections

the ground that crunches
beneath my feet
friends that i have yet to meet
those that have been there though it all
to share the highs
and cushion my falls
the words in which i've lost myself
different worlds picked off the shelf
music that has touched my soul
all the things that make me whole
the pen through which my truth has flowed
purpose found in stories told
connections to my deepest self
words released with hope they'll help
others that stumble along the way
and light the path that they must take
a lantern held by one that knows
however dark the journey
you are never alone

ways to wellbeing

feeling close to others
valued, needed, loved
caring, sharing, connected
belonging, a sense of 'us'

getting out and about, being active
nourishing body and soul
being at one with nature
on your marks, get set, go

being present in the moment
taking notice, being aware
of the sights and sounds around you
wherever you are, be there

challenging limitations
seeking new ways to grow
developing skills and learning
to where it might lead, who knows

and random acts of kindness
helping others in ways big and small
giving with no thought to what you'll get back
a better world for all

five simple ways to wellbeing
taking care of body and mind
a life of purpose and meaning
with so many reasons to smile

how winning is done

the race isn't won in just one day
away from the arena
we work, we train
preparing for when
opportunity comes
to grasp it, grab it
with both hands
and run
with it, give it
everything we have
believe there's no such thing
as can't

fortune favours the brave, the bold
life's a one-time deal
with no repeat shows
take your chances
by the scruff of the neck
never look back
with bitter regret

chase your dreams no matter what
don't surrender
never give in
and always remember
patience, my friend
life's a marathon not a sprint

nothing just happens

ain't no such thing as coincidence
no simple quirks of chance
there's design behind the random
we're performers in a cosmic dance

guided by an invisible hand
placing us where we should be
wherever it is we find ourselves
we can find opportunity

people cross our paths for a reason
teachers along the way
some forever some but for a season
until you know why
have faith

that one day hence you will realise
the gifts that each one brought
love, forgiveness, self-discovery
treasures that can't be bought

search for your passion, your purpose
the reason that you are alive
trust your instincts, follow your heart
for only then
will you fly

what would i write if i were dying

what would i write if i were dying
who would i speak to
what would i say
how many loose ends
would need to be tied
if my time were to come
today

what remnants would i leave behind
what burdens would i need to set free
to lighten my soul's final journey
and rest in peaceful sleep

when we're gone we leave only stories
traced within hearts that beat on
what would i write as the ink ran dry
and i arrived at my final full stop

mortality

as you pass through the gateway
from this world to the next
will there be words left unspoken
will you have given life your best
will you leave behind a legacy
of hearts filled with your love
shared while living life to the fullest
with no regrets and no what could
have beens had things been different
no what ifs clouding your past
no wondering where life would have led you
had you chosen a different path
will the tears that flow at your passing
be wiped away by grateful smiles
by those touched by your presence
will your memory never die
and when you make that final journey
what gifts will you leave behind
what will tell the world that you were here
when it's time to say goodbye

the boxes you put me in

i am a number
i am a passing memory
i am a painful lesson
and someone's regret

i am a pound sign
a mistake not to be repeated
a momentary pleasure
a means to an end
i am a tick in a box
an itch to be scratched
an interlude
a long ago chapter long since read

a puzzle that couldn't be solved
a hoped for future
consigned to the past
an expectation unfulfilled
a disposable bit of fun
a convenient salve

whatever it is
that i am to you
i
will define me

who cares what they think

who cares what they think
who cares how you look
who cares what you earn
who gives a fuck

who cares what they think
pay the critics no mind
looking down from their pedestals
judgemental, smug and snide

who cares what they think
and who are 'they' anyway
this invisible enemy
with nothing good to say

who cares what they think
those so quick to condemn
and why is it so many of us
put our worth in the hands of them

who gives a fuck what they think
get busy living your life for you
waste no energy on those that don't care
save it for those that do

golden thread

a future seen in glimpses
from a present
pieced together of parts
no longer looking
for a golden thread
that could never stretch
that far

to know what it is to be broken

to know what it is to be broken
to have been shrouded in a veil of black
to have reached the bottom of the dark abyss
not knowing how or if you'll climb back
to have found yourself in your lowest moments
lost and all alone
barely clinging onto
whatever is left to hold

to know what it is to be broken
to feel a fissure open inside
leaking out your identity
your dignity, your pride
sucked into a sinkhole
left dizzy from the spin
knowing only that you're broken
not knowing how to begin
to reassemble the pieces
of your dark and fractured mind
hoping, praying, begging
for a strength that you cannot find

when you know what it is to be broken
and from out of the wreckage you've climbed
when you've pieced yourself back together
it's time for a new you to rise

with strength hitherto unimagined
steel forged within fiery depths
wisdom won in the toughest of battles
that never will you forget
yet not to be carried as your burden
nor worn as some terrible flaw
for now you stand as the victor
having won an invisible war

pieces of me

there are many things in life i've been
many things that make me 'me'
a son, a brother, an employee
a husband once
again, maybe

a listening ear, a loyal friend
stubborn, headstrong, an imperfect blend
funny (sometimes), serious too
loud and talkative
quiet, subdued

easy-going, a passion for living
impatient, irritable, kind and giving
an open mind, a bruised heart
a writer
releasing pain through art

with every day, further becoming
who i am, embracing it fully
all i am, for good, for bad
best of all, will always
be dad

ABOUT THE AUTHOR

Matthew Williams is an author and speaker. He lives in the North East of England with his two children. He is passionate about positive change and turning life's challenges into lessons for creating a better future. He hopes that by sharing his own experiences he can inspire others to make positive changes in their lives.

A Familiar Stranger is his first poetry collection.

Something Changed: Stumbling Through Divorce, Dating & Depression is also available from Sixth Element Publishing

More of Matthew's writing can be found at his website, Love, Laughter, Truth www.lovelaughtertruthblog.com

You can follow Matthew on social media: Twitter: @3DMathW Facebook: /mwlovelaughtertruth/ Instagram: math_williams

Printed in Great Britain
by Amazon

84087193R00089